Materials, Material

Wood

Chris Oxlade

Heinemann Library
Chicago, Illinois

Designed by Storeybooks
Originated by Ambassador Litho Ltd.
Printed in Hong Kong / China

05 04 03 02 01
10 9 8 7 6 5 4 3 2

Library of Congress Cataloging-in-Publication Data

Oxlade, Chris.
  Wood / by Chris Oxlade.
      p. cm. -- (Materials, materials, materials)
Includes bibliographical references and index.
  ISBN 1-58810-158-4
  1. Wood--Juvenile literature. [1. Wood.] I. Title. II. Series.
  TA419 .O95 2001
  575.4' 6--dc21
                                        00-012894

Acknowledgments
The author and publishers are grateful to the following for permission to reproduce copyright material:
Oxford Scientific Films, pp. 4, 9, 10; Tudor Photography, pp. 5, 7, 14, 17, 20, 21; Holt, p. 6; The Builder Group, p. 8;
Still Pictures/Mark Edwards, p. 11; Still Pictures/Hartmut Schwarzbach, p. 12; Corbis/Barry Lewis, p. 13;
Photodisc, pp. 15, 26, 27; Trip/Viesti Collection, p. 18; Corbis, p. 19; Corbis/Richard T. Nowitz, p. 22; Hutchison, p.
23; Corbis/Darrell Gulin, p. 24; Oxford Scientific Films/Michael Fogden, p. 25; Corbis/Jack Fields, p. 29.

Cover photograph reproduced with permission of Robert Harding Picture Library.

Every effort has been made to contact copyright holders of any material reproduced in this book.
Any omissions will be rectified in subsequent printings if notice is given to the publisher.

Note to the Reader
Some words are shown in bold, **like this.**
You can find out what they mean by looking in the glossary.

Contents

What Is Wood?

branch

trunk

Wood comes from the **trunks** and **branches** of trees. It is a **natural** material. People cut down trees and chop them up for wood.

Wood is an important material.
People make many different things
from it. All the things in this picture
are made of wood.

Different Woods

Different parts of a tree have different kinds of wood. On the outside, the tree **trunk** and **branches** are covered with thick, rough **bark.** Inside the tree trunk, the wood has lines in it called rings.

Different trees have different kinds of wood. For example, beech trees are made of a hard, heavy wood. Balsa trees are made of a soft, light wood.

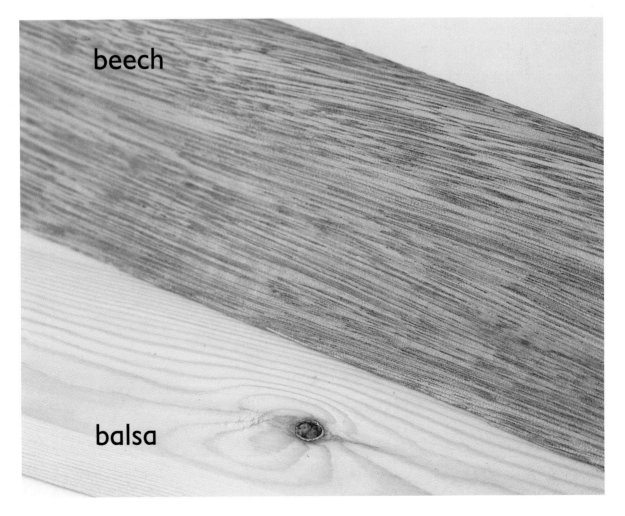

beech

balsa

Strong and Easy to Bend

Most kinds of wood are strong. Wood taken from the **trunk** of a tree is the strongest. Strong wood does not bend easily. This building is being made with thick pieces of strong, hard wood.

The young, thin **branches** of some trees bend easily. They can bend almost in half without snapping. This can be very useful for making things.

Rotting and Burning

When **branches** break off a tree and fall to the ground, the wood begins to **rot.** Water makes wood rot. This floor got too wet. It is rotting.

Wood does not **melt** when it is heated. It burns. People all over the world collect wood for **fuel.** They use it for cooking or for keeping warm.

Growing Wood

Much of the wood we use to build and
to make furniture comes from fir trees.
When the trees are big enough, they are
cut down. Then we can use the wood.

After trees are cut down, their
branches are cut off. The **trunks**
of the trees are taken to a **sawmill.**
They are cut into large, heavy boards.

Working with Wood

Wood is a useful material because it is easy to cut. A **carpenter** cuts and shapes wood to make things. Carpenters work with tools such as saws and drills.

This building is being made from wood. The carpenter cuts pieces of wood into different lengths with an electric saw. Then he joins the pieces together with nails and screws.

Sheets of Wood

Sheets of wood are called boards. **Chipboard** is made of small chunks of wood. The chunks are mixed with glue and squeezed together until the glue hardens.

Plywood is another kind of board. It is made by gluing thin sheets of hard wood on top of each other. Plywood is very strong and lasts a long time.

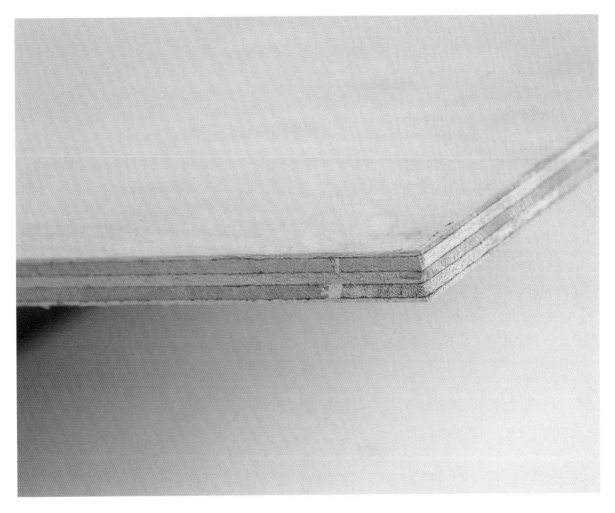

Caring for Wood

Wood used outside has to be kept from **rotting.** People cover wood with layers of thick, oily paint. This keeps water from soaking into it.

Fence posts are dipped in special **chemicals.** Then they are put in the ground. The chemicals keep the fence posts from rotting.

Patterns in Wood

The patterns in wood **grain** can be very beautiful. People make wood smooth by rubbing it with **sandpaper.** Then they polish the wood to make the grain stand out.

Different colors of wood can be put next to each other to make patterns. This wood vase has a pattern of smaller pieces of wood.

Local Wood

Some people live in places where there are large forests. They use wood for most of the things they build. Log cabins are built from whole tree **trunks.**

Sometimes, people make boats from tree trunks. They dig out the center of the trunk. Then they shape the rest of it into a boat. These boats are called dugouts.

Animals That Use Wood

Many animals use wood to build, too. Beavers cut down trees with their sharp front teeth. They use the wood to build **dams** and homes called lodges.

Many birds make nests from **branches** that they find on the ground. The male bowerbird in Australia builds an **arch** over his nest. He uses branches and grass.

Saving the Rain Forests

Rain forests are full of huge, old trees. They are an important part of the world because many kinds of animals live there. People cut down thousands of rain forest trees for wood every day.

One way to help save rain forest trees is to plant new trees. We can cut down trees we have planted when we need wood. Then we will not need to cut down any rain forest trees.

Fact File

▶ Wood comes from trees. It is a **natural** material.

▶ Wood from a tree feels rough.

▶ Woods from different kinds of trees are different colors. Wood has a pattern in it called the **grain.**

▶ Some kinds of wood are heavy and hard. Some kinds are light and soft.

▶ Thick pieces of wood are stiff. Thin pieces of wood bend easily.

▶ Wood burns when it is heated.

▶ Wood floats in water.

▶ Wood is not attracted by **magnets.**

▶ **Electricity** and heat do not flow through wood.

Can You Believe It?

The biggest airplane in the world is made completely of wood! It was built in 1947 and is called the *Spruce Goose*. It is even bigger than a modern jumbo jet!

Glossary

arch curved part of something

bark rough, outer layer of a tree trunk or branch

branch limb of a tree

carpenter person who works with wood to make things

chemical material used to clean or protect something

chipboard small chunks of wood mixed with glue and squeezed together to make a board

dam something built to hold back water

electricity form of power that can light lamps, heat houses, and make things work

fuel something that people burn to make heat or light or to make engines work

grain pattern of rings and lines in wood

magnet piece of iron or steel that pulls steel and iron things toward it

melt turn from solid to liquid

natural comes from plants, animals, or rocks in the earth

rain forest thick, jungle-like forest where lots of rain falls

rot to fall apart because of dampness

sandpaper tough paper with sand glued to it that is used to make wood smooth

sawmill factory where trees are cut into boards with powerful saws

trunk main part of a tree

More Books to Read

Burby, Liza N. *A Day in the Life of a Carpenter.* New York: Rosen, 1999.

Chambers, Catherine. *Wood.* Austin, Tex.: Raintree Steck-Vaughn, 1996.

Madgwick, Wendy. *Super Materials.* Austin, Tex.: Raintree Steck-Vaughn, 1999.

Royston, Angela. *Life Cycle of an Oak Tree.* Chicago: Heinemann Library, 2000

Index